THE VISITANTS

Poetry by Miriam Waddington

MIRIAM WADDINGTON

THE VISITANTS

Toronto
OXFORD UNIVERSITY PRESS
1981

Grateful acknowledgement is made to the Canada Council and to editors of the following magazines where some of these poems first appeared: *Aurora, Canadian Forum, NeWest Review, Queen's Quarterly, Saturday Night, Tamarack Review, This Magazine, Toronto Life, Room of One's Own, Waves,* and to *CBC Anthology.*

To the memory of my mother
Mussia Dobrushin Dworkin

Canadian Cataloguing in Publication Data

Waddington, Miriam, 1917-
    The visitants

Poems.
ISBN 0-19-540380-0

I. Title.

√ PS8545.A32V57   C811'.54   C81-095019-7
PR9199.3.W3V57

34,595

CONTENTS

Contents

I. CONSERVING

Why does woman always come into the class of evil, dangerous, and less valuable? —Otto Rank

PLAYING

Let's fly
be blue as air
fall off the
world weightless
and wayless;

Or crackle
like paper explode
into ho-ho-hey-hey
flowers and
rustle like

Leaves hide
from cats leap
into squirrel nests
or hang from
tree-swings;

Then climb
up high wires
down jim-jams
and plant red
and blue

Maps on the
baby continents,
then let's rock
those small
continents

in their blue
sky cradles to a
gentle laughing
sleep.

CONSERVING

On November afternoons
the harem girls are out
walking their dogs.

They have eaten pineapples
and drunk white wine,
they have heard murmurings

From enchanted palaces,
they have dreamed of sultans
with turbans of gold.

The frost pinches their faces,
the wind teases their hair,
their eyes have the blinds down,

They don't want anyone to see
behind their shuttered eyes
where they are working hard

To conserve the small heat
in the rooms of their lives;
they are husbanding warmth

For their annointed lords
who will return from travels
at difficult sundown,

After dangerous journeys
on highways and throughways,
after hand-to-hand fighting

In offices and corridors;
what more can harem girls do?
They have walked their dogs

And eaten the pineapples,
they have combed out their hair
and buffed up their nails,

They have chopped up the day
for firewood, hating November,
and now they are burning the sultans

With the turbans of gold,
they are burning their dreams
in suburban fireplaces.

Perhaps the harem girls are angry,
for it is not always possible
to be beautiful or to walk the dogs;

And they have to work so hard,
they have to burn more dreams
than they really have

In order to conserve the heat
in the small rooms
where they live.

THE BIG TREE

I dreamed
the big tree
in my backyard
was being chopped
down by blades
dropping from
aeroplanes sent by
the prime minister
of remote control
from the province
of pipelines and
the land of final
solutions.

At dawn the
planes flew past
my house
dropping salt
to seed rain and
spraying Zen-X
to dissolve
the ozone.

Somewhere
underground Lot
looked up from
his forge with
a red steaming
face and roared
out above the
fiery noise:

This is what
comes of all
your know-how,
everyone will
burn anyhow
and equally in
the empty
emptiness and

There will be
no one left
to inscribe
even a single
little hieroglyph
on the age-old
pillar of salt.

THE MILK OF
THE MOTHERS

Stars, stars,
lean down and speak:
tell me what I am
on mother earth,
our planet.

They have reduced
our winnowing skies
to ash and lava,
and set out lunar
onion plants with
mountain parsley;
without a word they
rolled our mother
earth, this planet,
in syrups of the dead.

Crumbs of recent
feudal feasts
still cling to our
nuclear shrouds,
and one-dimensional
graphic cows are
outlined stiff in
charcoal to mark
the shadowy shifting
negatives of field
and forest.

No grave
delineates the light
of absent earth,
and there is no one
left to hear
the cries of those
whose ashes are
heaped green and
pulsing in deserted
tomato fields.

Tell me, stars,
what fortune-teller
will now guess
the thoughts of
weather and what
wizard bind the
splintered sides
of logged-over
blackened hills?

Stars, the milk
of the old mothers
is thin and the
milk of the young
mothers is shrieking;
the milk of the
mothers runs out
from every eye and
breast and throbs
with the white blood
of electricity.

Stars, stars,
lean down and speak!
Tell me what I am,
and tell me where
is the milk of
all the mothers now
on earth, our planet?

HONOURING HEROES

In April he stands
narrow-chested and tall
in a net of bare branches,
he is saying goodbye
before he leaves
on one of his journeys,
his forehead is as tanned
as any explorer's,
and around him are many
beautiful women all
with the same face.

Does he know
that even explorers
grow older and lose
their hair while the
beautiful women stay
always the same, young
hipless and windblown,
with the same fixed
empty eyes?

Sometimes he feels
the flow of his blood
shifting and shrinking,
or his heart turning grey
and beginning to crumble;
has anyone counted
the lands he has surveyed,
the tombs he has rifled,
or even how many lions
he has shot with that
mounting courage so much
admired and envied?
How many wives has he had,
and how many children
has he abandoned and buried?

When you go to shake his hand
you see a tiny blood speck
floating in his left eye,
so small it is hardly
noticeable yet you see it
and recognize it,
it is the stigma of a wound
nothing can heal,
it will grow and spread,
it will devour his life.

FEASTS

Beside the sandy
road and the historic
river three Indian
boys from a lost
prairie are eating
their lunch,
they have come here
to hunt but we
have come here to
cut spruce boughs
for the Feast of
the Tabernacles.

The maple trees
are burning fiercely,
their red and yellow
leaves ignite the
Sunday afternoon
and their redness
bites into us,
points us winterward
to December nights
lighted only by
snow trees from
the Gatineau.

SOUTH AMERICAN NIGHTS

She dreams she is
queen of a brothel
in a wide feather-bed,
her name was lost
in some prison and
now they call her
      Rose Red.

She loves the cruel
prince of a burnt-out
war-surplus shed, his
subjects are armless
guerillas and their
camp is a starved
      river bed.

She dances with green
mercenaries and
garbage bags stuffed
with the dead,
she dreams she is
queen of a brothel
and her name is
      Rose Red.

PRIMARY COLOURS

1. BEING BORN

Be red,
a red of space
and stretch,
a flow,
a burst of
burn.

And now
reverse, contract,
enclose
to interpoint:
shift darkness
into out or in
until you have
a hearse,
a box, a cage,
with nets and loops
of leaves, with pods
of seeds.

Then move
in protoplasmic
dance
through streaming
mysteries
of cell and cellicle;
flow
through careful
barriers of bone
and storms
of blood,
past cartilage

and hinge,
past loose vestigial
wings and
dangle from torn
ligaments and broken
muscle strings.

Whatever
you are or ever
were or who,
made old or
born new,
embellish,
polish space;
rake up the
summer, loosen
winds,
plant seeds until
glorious at last
you hang
upside down from
sky's umbilicals.

2. LIVING

Be blue,
a blue of fathomless,
a spray of far,
a gleam of
absent sunlit
highs and
glittering echoings,
grab the empty
edge of skies,
swing wide,
and plunge
to blanching
presences.

Now write
your hieroglyphs
on snowman's
letterhead,
dictate
your glaciers to
sleeping space,
compose
an orange song
and circle it
with canticles
of blue;
pack up the forest
and consign
its hundred owlish
eyes to earth
in nailed crates
of night.

Or slide
some measured
two-by-fours
through open
window frames;
then wake the
dreaming dead
and touch
their breath
with stars.

Before you leave,
sweep the blue
sawdust up
into a heap,
and with clean
brushes scatter it—
through a thousand
radiant doors.

3. DYING

Yellow,
who are you
yellow?
Tuwhit tuwhoo
I am I,
yellow and
you are you.

Yellow
you are the
sound's horizons,
its early
orisons unpacked
from vats
of dew.

And yellow,
you are the
golden bar
across
the topmost
star.

You are also
the fertile toad
of the yellow
swollen day,
you are yellow;
the shrunken
pearl of the
loudly yellow
night.

SELVES

1

My old self
comes back
to visit me
more and more
often; at three
years old at
four years old,
at six years old.

I am three,
I am sitting
on a brown floor
holding a mirror
in broken sunlight,
I squint at my face
in the mirror it is
derelict streaked
with tears.

My hair what is
left of it is
ragged, the scissors
are still open in
my hand and my
tears are falling
through the spaces
between the sun-bars
that open and close
like shutters on
the floor.

I am crying,
I will be scolded,
I will be punished,
I will be ugly
duckling and my
uncle will never
make spinners out
of buttons and string
for me again.

My mother will stand
towering over me,
made of huge marble,
a naked statue,
like the one on the
postcards people are
always sending us
from the Louvre.

2

I am four years old;
my mother among
the picnic things
is calling: *Mia, Mia,
Mia!* I hear her but
I wait till she turns
her back, I am there
all the time right
under her nose buried
in last autumn's leaves.

As soon as her back
is turned I jump up
and throw off the leaves,
I run north, Kildonan
Park is empty as a
theatre on Monday
morning and the tall
elms are pillars
holding up the sky.

I keep on running,
I'm heading for
Dead Man's Creek,
I run past notches
cut into the bark,
I plunge through
mushroom dust and
fern jungles, I blanch
I am afraid, what if
I meet a giant or
a witch, or worse—
what if I meet the
dark chloroform lady
who waits behind the
door of the cupboard
in my room, or most
terrifying of all
the Selkirk avenue
streetcar conductor
with the big loud
buttons?

3

At six years old
I can still hear
my mother's voice
calling, *Mia, Mia,*
but I don't care,
she doesn't own me,
I'm running away
going to the forest
still heading for
Dead Man's creek,
still looking for
buried treasure.

Suppose I get there
and am the first to
find it, what then?
Three boys once went
fishing from the banks
of the Red River they
found a dead gopher
and started to bury it,
they dug a hole and
found treasure, an iron
box full of gold coins
left there by pirates
or other explorers.

I find only
a handful of dandelions,
but I feel
just as rich.

PRAIRIE

The only
shadows here
are those of
angels soft
and ruffled as
paper flowers
in the churches
of the poor.

These shadows
settle like
wings on either
side of a
giant seed.

HOLIDAY POSTCARDS

I meant to send you
a postcard but the
farmer came out of
his dell and went
commercial the scene
changed old Mother
Goose was forced out
of the fairy-tale
business nursery
rhymes were passé
too tame not enough
blood hyperactivity
or brain damage not
enough how shall I
put it old men with
young women young
men with old women
battered wives or
suicidal husbands
and the sharks were
after everybody.

Nature was
all disordered
the zucchini always
overcooked the wine
tasting of tar and
even my good friend
the wind blowing hot
and cold and never
knowing which way
to turn: everything
was crazy and I

couldn't find the
right kind of
postcard showing
what it was really
like to go on holiday
five thousand miles
from home only to
see that everything
was exactly the same
there as here.

That was my big
discovery the farmer
going commercial
kicking the cat loading
the donkey taking his
wife locking up the
house selling it to
developers and going
into a new kind of
retirement condominium
that was just being
built in Delphi or
maybe it was Florida but
honest I meant to
send you a postcard
telling about the
grass at least and
the flowers whose names
you know and the
ocean that was blue
and still tasted so
miraculously of salt.

UNEMPLOYMENT TOWN

Even here
the children look
up from their
sandboxes to smile
briefly into
the camera.

The icy villages
and empty harbours
are back there
behind them wrapped
in the loitering
streets, washed in
the civic fountains
and the thin dreams
of their shivering
fathers.

It is all there
inside the camera
under the torn
clothes and the
forlorn gutters,
and especially
in the pieces of
old rope left
lying around on
roads that always
lead nowhere.

HISTORY: IN JORDAN

Long ago
you drowned
in the lake
of my sleep.

I buried you
in a tomb
in faraway Egypt,
in Cairo's crumbling
city of the dead.

You don't remember;
you have forgotten
the long paved streets
and the burst water pipes
of Jarash.

As for the amphitheatre
and the Nubian actress
who was homesick for Crete,
you kissed her in the wings
where the wind was
the only voice.

The wind and
the silence
and the bent grass
that grows
between stones.

I too have forgotten
that time.

LETTER FROM EGYPT

In this country
noon
embroiders night
with golden
threads
and the stars
leave their love
messages in
hollow skies.

The forests
are full of the
noise of priests
at their prayers,
but the rabbis
have all gone away;
they rode out
one long-ago day
on their own
nightmares.

And guess what?
The people all
live in the tombs,
they have chopped
down the trees
and killed the
caterpillars, then
they watered
the sands, poisoned
their hens and dyed
oceans the colour
of Macbeth's
plunging hands.

They also speak
a strange language
here, so don't buy
your ticket just yet;
if you come you
may not be met,
the taxis have all
gone to war
and the fields
are drowning in sand.

Wherever you look
things crumble and
break and even my
cymbals don't ring;
of course nobody
dances and the
pyramids still
aren't built, so
wait till you hear
that we have our
visas for home.

Until then
I don't think
you would like it
here.

WARNINGS

Don't fall in love
with that face!
It looks older
and kinder but
it's the face
of your husband
long dead with
flowers in his
eyes and grasses
in his hair
so beware!
Beware of the
cruel animal
lurking there
(his heart is
its lair.)

Don't fall in love
with that face!
You, the stranger and
walker-at-leisure,
are in danger, in
danger! You'll slide
slow as glaciers
through old arctic
passes where ice-
palms wave their

fringes above cream-
coloured bears and
the seals dive
down to explore the
tusky deeps under
bluebeard's locked
door, where the black
oil gushes your death
from the bluest fjords
of your sleep.

It's there
that you'll drown
in the flowers and
choke on the grasses,
there that you'll
lose your way in
the maze of antarctic
passes, and you'll
freeze (how you'll
freeze!) in the
windblack meadows
of ice on far frozen
northern seas, so
don't fall in love
with that face!

A GOOD MAN
AND A PASSIONATE WOMAN

A good man
has little need
of a passionate woman
he is so timely so finely
balanced he is
a reservoir
filled to the brim
with good water as
good as himself,
he is pure and
fine-toned, tautening
as chokecherry juice
and careful as a ripe
leaf about which hill
he rolls over but

The passionate woman
poor thing she walks
her precarious balance
on the wobbliest wires
she might be
electrocuted and whether
she knows who cares and
whether she cares

who knows, she is
fuzzy and half-asleep
in summer and in
winter the wind is
her cold comforter
her sole printer.

Still she sees
into reservoirs deep
enough to find
reflections,
she admires the rare
goodness of the
good man she
dangles his good
profile like a drowner's
medal and she lets
his cleft chin divide
the whole autumn and
half-asleep
she hears how his
goodness sounds
in the faraway valleys
of spring.

CERTAIN WINTER

I am still
as a bird
(the winter
shakes snow down
trembles
is space)

The world rises
and sinks
bewitched and
entranced under
skyspeeds
and cloudwands,
trees rise and
turn, then sink
to snow blindness
coiling their
silence
in spiralling
roots

(Where is the swanboat
of Lohengrin of Leda,
of the crystalline
Elsa who waits for
a name?
Who launched their
letters like ships
on the waters, hung
questions on sedges,
then braided the
daisies to wires
of ice?)

(To love her to
knot her the king's
only daughter,
soon is too late
now Apollo has caught
her, and sealed her
and wound her around
in her fate; three
stems and a flower
two wings and
a seed)

Stems of love
seeds of light
touch me and
tremble, they
fold away darkness
in the nests of
last autumn
(I am still
as a bird
in a world
entranced)

HOROSCOPES

I was born
in winter the
December of
revolution but
my lovers were
all from autumn,
scorpios and
sagittarians
sourpusses and
vegetarians.

Now I await
the true lover
omened by stars
and promised
by rain,
he will come
with his bow
and his arrow
dressed in the
green livery
of spring.

II. HOW OLD WOMEN SHOULD LIVE

. . . Time itself
Shall much befriend you
—William Cowper

CRAZY TIMES

When the birds riot
and the airplanes walk,
when the busy sit,
and the silent talk;

When the rains blow
and the winds pour,
when the sky is a land
and the sea its shore;

When shells grow snails
and worms eat toads,
when winters chase summers
on upside-down roads,

We'll sit by our fires
and warm our hands,
and tell old tales
of bygone lands.

HOW OLD WOMEN SHOULD LIVE

Old women
should live like worms
under the earth,
they should come out
only after a good rain.

Or be the kind of worm
that lives in flour
that has stood too long
and when discovered
is thrown away in disgust
by the good housewife.

Or be a wood-worm
that patiently winds
its journey through
history's finest
furniture like those
old women we see
in the corridors of
nursing homes.

Or they should be
constructive like the
silk-worm who lives
on nothing but a box
of mulberry leaves in
hot China too far away
to bother anyone.

The wisest old women
imitate the glow-worm
who is never seen by day
with all its grey worminess
and shrivelled feet,
but shines wise and warm
only after dark.

Old women should be
magical like those worms
in transition and chrysalis
from egg to butterfly;
even decrepit old women
can turn into butterflies
in the third existence
promised to us all.

And remember that worms
are fussy about where
they live and what they eat;
they like warmth, darkness,
and good nourishment and
sometimes when it suits them
they like to come out in
all their loose nakedness
to crawl in the sun.

OLD AGE BLUES

This is an age
where you have to
expect disasters;
in summer the roof
leaks in winter the
balcony collapses
under the weight
of snow and the
furnace also gives
up the ghost, coughs
and sneezes, finally
explodes in a fury
of old age so
sing, sing the blues.

Even worse: the man
you thought would
marry you marries
someone else (lady
your house is more
than 20 years old
you've been getting
a free ride no repairs
all these years) and
your youth is more
than 20 years away so
sing, sing the blues.

Also, move along:
can't you see that
the sidewalks are
crowded and the
throughways are
throbbing with the
rutting young and
jumping with *No
Exit* signs? They
say that old wood
burns slowly but
old wisdom never
made anyone's heart
burn brighter so
goodbye now and
sing, sing the blues.

Here I go, flying
high, disguised as
a fairy godmother
whirling and twirling
my old-age wand;
just watch me—
I'm about to turn
a million glittering
cartwheels in milky
outer skies and I'm
rolling in stars,
rolling all the way
up to eternity and
I'm singing
sing, sing the blues.

PORTRAIT OF THE
OWNER OF A
SMALL GARBAGE CAN

The woman who
lives alone has
only a small-size
garbage can to put
out Monday mornings,
very little garbage
and very few leaves
to rake; the leaves
fall in profusion
only in yards where
children play.

The single woman
is lucky if the sun
shines on her and
the wind blows
through her hair,
the touch of the
wind the touch of
the sun even the
bite of frost is
the closest she
will ever come
to knowing love.

Instead of kisses
what she gets are
lonely dinners in
vegetarian restaurants,
under the sugary
lights of the icy
chandeliers in a
chain eating-house
she dances every
night with a different
steak made of nutmeats
and eggplant.

She walks back
through the streets
of an empty Toronto,
her tongue feels
deep-fried, her glass
slippers hurt and
she has lost the
telephone number of
the fairy prince.

At home she goes
upstairs and lays out
next day's clothes,
then she fills
a hot-water bottle
shaped like a toad,
sighs pearls and
goes to bed.

WHEN THE SHOE
IS ON THE OTHER FOOT
FOR A CHANGE

Fall in love?
I can't you're
too old your
body is cold,
your life runs
away like water
off clay your
body is dry
as old bread,
your hands spidery
red your lips
mouldy and grey,
your words are
heavy, unleavened
as lead and you
smell of death
and decay.
Get lost, shoo, vamoose,
go away.

REAL ESTATE:
POEM FOR VOICES

Life begins enclosed, protected, all warm
in the bosom of the house. —Gaston Bachelard

Alone in a house
between two cities
she was living
the story of centuries;
note this: that year
birds outroared
the traffic
YOU BETTER BELIEVE IT

A flowering
snail
one breast one
hand and the
shadow woman,
a stamenless calyx
in a garden
of grasses
WE COULDN'T CARE LESS

That year the
summer hours fell
just short of
twilight in a
spring of humid
dawns and cuspidors,
and there was
nothing to suggest
lilacs or the
smell of syringa
ALL THAT BULLSHIT

The hours
continued to be
empty as sucked-out
honeycomb and
transparent as
dragonfly wings
or bluebottles
making their speedo-
whizz getaways
(watch out for
those dragonflies
they're really
darning needles who
sew your mouth up)
WHAT BOOK DID YOU
READ THAT IN?

The hours
continued to be
bland and mean
as city neighbours,
their car exhausts
everyone's serenade,
their dogdroppings
everyone's carpet,
their lawnmowings
everyone's banquet
SO LET THEM EAT GRASS

Half-woman
purpling in the
shadow of the
shadow woman,
if you could only
tell fortunes or
read oracles or
have a good car-
washing husband
WHY DON'T YOU GO BACK
WHERE YOU CAME FROM?

It is completely
irrelevant to ask
what is your house of
spruce saying over
and over again and
what is the message
of pine over and over
again and what is
the burden of beech
over and over again
and how about the
agony of elm over
and over again
GO HIRE A HALL

And if it's answers
you want
cheerful answers
if you insist,
the developers
have changed the
by-laws, you must
start packing
now this minute;
if you refuse and
are still here
tomorrow they'll
take and shoot you
HURRY UP TIME
IS MONEY

One hand
one breast
a shadow-woman,
maybe one
is better than
none, who says
a snail needs
a shell a bird
its nest we must
fight to stay
alive we must
fight fight
THAT'S ALL RIGHT
DON'T MENTION IT

PAST THE ICE AGE

All of a sudden
I was empty spaces,
flexible snow
wrapping the air.

All of a sudden
I was ropes of night,
crickets of song
under cellar stairs.

I was a lap of
strawberries a stand
of cornflowers a
glassful of ice

And I wanted to
live a long time
just to hear
the new music
in everything.

COMMITTEES

All the outpatients
of Toronto have
overnight become patrons
of life; they have been
elected to committees
on longevity, they sit in
special clinics studying
their horoscopes convinced
there is a science as
well as a strategy to this
business of outwitting the
scowling doctor of death.

RUNNING UP AND DOWN
MOUNTAINS AT CHANGING SPEEDS

Fifteen years ago
it was my pleasure to run
up and down the mountain
in Montreal; not only pleasure
but ecstasy, and I knew
what the word meant;
I used to open my arms
to the wind, be embraced
by a huge wave of air, then
enclosed in a cape of the
same air with only my head
showing and only my voice
sounding; I used to shout
to the sky: *hey, look world—*
world, here I am!

And in those days
the sky did look at me
half-approving and half-
disapproving, and the trees
inclined to each other and
whispered: *psst there she is!*
And the wind shouted back
at me: *look who just blew in!*
and all of us together
raised our voices in a choir
of hallelujahs singing the
same song to each other and
to the world about the
pleasures of running up
and down mountains.

These days I sometimes
give a little secret run
when no one is looking,
I might even bend over and
pick a late dandelion or
out-of-season clover from
a south-facing ditch, and
I always stop to listen to
a bird calling another bird,
wondering what they are
saying with their bird-talk:
that the worm crop is good,
that we need more rain,
that someone's nest just
fell out of a tree, or what?

Whatever they are saying
they will never get the
chance to say about me
that it is one of the sins
of my old age to pretend
I'm still running up and down
mountains the way I used to.
I acknowledge my bad temper,
short breath and all my
disappointments: these days
I don't have the nerve anymore
to shout up at the sky: *Look,
here I am world!* These days
I'm glad of every small
courtesy, I rejoice when
the wind steps aside for
me and greets me quietly
with cheeks puffed down
and lips unpursed, and I
like it when he whispers:
*hello old friend, so you're
still here!*

LADY IN BLUE:
HOMAGE TO MONTREAL

Lady in the blue
dress with the
sideward smile,
I see you at your
easel in the field
beside your house
painting the blur
of long-ago summer
in the night-eyes
of children in the
dark mouths of
sleepwalkers in the
floating bodies
of rock-throwers
and flame-eaters.

In the soundless
streets of our French
bedlam city with
its old creaking
heart and venereal
stairways, its bridges,
spaghetti houses, railway
hotels and second-hand
monuments, there,
Lady Blue of the
saint suburbs, there,

just there you were
lost, lost under
the mountain, under
the snows and calèches,
the steep cliffs of
Côte des Neiges, there
you were lost under
the fortress façades
of a thousand steel-
armoured apartments.

Under the slow blonde
sorrows of your tangled
hair we are all lost,
lost in the distance of
endless streets in the
trackless wastes of our
vanished mother-city;
we are ghost people,
uneasy night-walkers
locked up in Montreal,
and we will never leave
unless your tireless
brush moves us and draws
us into the blue-sleeved
avenues of your still-
flowing rivery wonder.

OLD WOMAN IN A GARDEN

There she is
kneeling in the garden,
an old woman
planting tomatoes,
sifting the earth,
breaking the clay,
her face half-hidden
by a red garden hat.

There she is
old woman in a garden,
satisfied with the sun,
not wondering
how long he will stay,
knowing
he can't go away
or die like
the others.

He won't
grow up or go
away he will always
be yellow-eyed
and young
with a honey tongue
and a bee-striped smile,
he can't go away,
he is here to stay,
and every morning
he brings her
a breakfast tray
with a cupful of light
and a saucer of day.

There she is
kneeling in the garden,
an old woman
in a red garden hat;
what is she thinking of
as she scratches the earth
and plants her few
small seeds?

CELEBRATING MAVERICKS

Go little words and fly,
round up the mavericks
all those stranger-words
and make of your flight
a moving wing of sound,
a deepening of the
ever-darkening light.

Advance, but curb the
changing words with reins,
bells, fringes, tassels and
soft bandages; with them
you'll bind angels, jokes,
gabby citizens, seed-lists,
and people raking leaves.

Then, little words, expand,
be horticulturists, invent
new cabbages, grow roses, name
gentians for their blue and
coax low nasturtiums into
giant forest trees, lay out
rich gardens for the starving
world—water and fertilize.

Having done your work
lie down to rest in shade,
let ministers of sleep
lull you to dreaming and
when you wake find yourself
a marcher on parade,
an eternal member of some
other-world procession,
a golden cipher
in God's motorcade.

III. THE VISITANTS

The body calls it death.
—William Butler Yeats

THE TRANSPLATED:
SECOND GENERATION

Some day my son
you'll go to Leningrad,
you'll see grey canals
under arches and bridges,
you'll see green and white
walls of winter palaces,
you'll visit the towered
prison across the river
and smell the breath
of dead revolutions;
perhaps you'll even hear
the ghostly marching of
sailors in empty avenues
and catch the ebbing sound
of their wintry slogans.

You'll remember
that Jews could spend no
nights in Leningrad when
it was called St Petersburg;
Jews moved with documents
shuffled and crushed like
paper; the Yiddish writer
Peretz was met by his friend
Anski at Leningrad station;
he delivered his lecture
to a crowded hall then spent
the night in a suburb
twenty miles away.

Some day my son
when you are in Leningrad
you'll see those palaces
and turning fountains,
you'll stare at pendulums
of gilded saintliness,
count kingly treasure-hoards
in glass museum-cases;
then you'll remember
Nova Scotia's pasture lands
its clumps of blueberries
and our August mornings
on hidden lakes at the end
of logging roads.

And some day my son
just there in Leningrad
across those distances
you will feel my Winnipeg:
its lakes of fish its skies
of snow and its winds of
homelessness will stir
something in your blood;
then will you hear forgotten
languages and you will read
the troubled map of our
long ancestral geography
in your own son's eyes.

MANAGING DEATH

It is not easy
to manage death
or the thought of
death, our own or
that of our friends;
each friend who dies
empties the world
and leaves fainter
traces of our own
bodies on earth.

It is not easy
to manage death but
it is not heroic
either; it is the
piecemeal following
of hints, the slow
breaking of this
link or that in
the last quickening
flash of the iron
chain of the flesh.

It is moving through
the patchwork of light
into deepening darkness,
and the glimpsing against
our will of the land
that can only be known
by those who are silent
and blind.

THE VISITANTS

At night you think
of your friends the dead;
they sing to you
in a choir of stone voices
and you want to tell them
old stories more ancient
than you mortally know,
all that you fleetingly
surmise shimmering
through the hole
in the foliage of the
nearest tree.

Oh those voices of stone!
Those earth-stained voices
those murmurings in wood
those singings in grasses
those soundings and turnings
on the pathless prairie;
my father groaning and
Gabriel Dumont staring
blindly into the camera
of his own fate.

Those anguished visitants:
they come to dissolve
the emptiness,
they come to console
your cries they come
with their firefly lanterns
to lead you amazed
through their blazing
gateways of stone.

THE SECRET-KEEPER

In memory of Marvin Duchow

Long ago one April
you whispered and gave me
a secret to keep
of time and of music.

I pondered the secret,
and wrapped it in sleep,
then I put it away
forty years deep.

When you died I awoke
and pulled up the blinds,
I parted the clouds
and looked out into May.

What was the secret?
It was about being
young and about being
old and also about

The dying of Yeats
who came to Montreal and
sang of golden nut-trees
and of silver pears.

In June you came to visit
and played Mozart under
my window and in July
we met again and walked

On the royal mountain
with its fiery cross
and daytime blaze
of ponds and children.

You asked me why I knew
nothing about Bach but
I had no answer and stared
dumbly at swallows flying.

In August I stayed home
and when I looked up from
weeding the garden I swear
I heard Beethoven humming.

In September it rained:
there were storms in Europe
and Jews were in a hurry
to pack their belongings.

The rest of the world
was busy listening to the
overture of the death camps
in the music of Wagner.

In October there was no sun,
people said they had never
known the streets so empty
and the hospitals so full.

In November a miracle:
the azaleas flowered again,
we lighted lamps and had
second thoughts about leaving.

December was full of laser
lights and people picking
bouquets of pink sugar roses
off tall wedding cakes.

January was freeze-up time,
our father winter came and
wrapped us snugly in the fugues
of his cold white beard.

We slept through February
and only woke up when the
postman brought us valentines
stamped and postmarked *Death*.

In March we shovelled snow,
and then it was April again
after the thumpings of winter,
and the false alarms of spring.

Now at last I have found
what you gave me to keep,
the secret is simple,
and its music is this:

Dark night; pestilence.
A scabby apple tree.
Distorted song; its murmur
stilled; your death.
An empty field.

WHEN WE MET

When we met
the first time it was
really the last time,
we spoke to each other
in the lost tongues of
our parents' Europe;
whose piano did you play
that spring afternoon
in the shadowed house
near the mountain
and whose song was
I singing entirely
to myself?

Was I my mother?
Were you your father?
Did we meet on a street
in Odessa or a birch forest
on the Volga or was it at
the artificial lake I dug out
in miniature and planted round
with tall buttercups for trees
behind an old hotel
in Winnipeg?

Why did it take me
so long to find our
lost languages,
to learn our songs?

THE GREEN CABIN

The year went by
in marriages and deaths,
not least do I mourn
the death of my youth and
the death of
the friends of my youth,
and now at last I have begun
to mourn the death
of my young mother whose life
was bewildered by children,
and also to mourn the death
of the young mother in me
who still wanders so
restlessly haunting the lives
of her children.

In this year of deaths
and marriages I mourn
the death of the lover
in me who ran to meet
a world full of love and
star-blessed miracles,
but now those doors are shut,
and the miserly world
has locked all the rainbows
in earth.

Where did the year go
with all its marriages and
deaths, its wedding cakes
and funeral flowers?
How did the year drift out
on elegies and sail away
to foreign harbours before we
noticed its going?
Why did we continue to work
after our friends and lovers
died? Some of us sculpted
statues and others composed
life-music to each small
delicate motion while the rest
kept on painting people
in deck chairs staring out
at the never-ending sea.

This year of marriages
and deaths I sit and mourn
in the green cabin
under the spruce tree,
I hear the rain on the roof
black and dark as the heart
of November, a rain dark as
the heart of old age, dark
as my heart of stone that
mourns the dark stone of
age, itself a dark stone
in a dark dark age.

IN A SUMMER GARDEN

In memory of Morris Surdin

The musicians
who sang to us are dead;
they left us sitting alone
under the pear tree
in the scalding afternoons
of August; all at once
they emptied the garden
of sound and everything
stopped; even the wasps
hung motionless.

We still hear them,
those musicians who sang,
suspended they move
through the widening rings
of their silence until
they float in the leaves;
laughing and rosy-faced
they climb up to the sun
and turn the key of C
in the door of the sky,
they stand on a threshold
of clouds and throw down
capfuls of sound, rich
and shining as cherries.

The musicians who died
are still singing and laughing,
they are whirling and dancing
in the spiralling wind
to the tune of new songs;
their notes shiver the clouds;
their voices are saying
they want us to sing.

ELEGIES FOR
A COMPOSER

1

Now there is only
the whisper of grass,
gentle under the flight
of your song's swallow.

Now there is only
the motion of earth that
sleeps under the mountain
beyond your song's sorrow.

2

You have crossed
into the world
below the frost line,
you have gone to join
the effigies of
our immigrant parents
who lie frozen
into statues under
fields of snow.

They lie there
and wait for us
under the wild sage
of their summer,
they look out at us
from the hundred white
eyes of the stinkweed
that grows so modestly
on the prairie.

Muffled by mouthfuls
of earth their voices
sing to us in the lost
tongues of our childhood,
they sing to us
the buried truth
of ourselves.

3

Why did it take us
a lifetime to hear
through the strange
accents of our parents
our own songs?

4

Now you are dead
and your song is
digging its way up
through the garden;
it emerges slow and
glistening with the
earthworms who labour
so earnestly for every
new planting.

BULGARIAN SUITE

1

Shall we sing of the graves
in the forest of tombstones
in the museum village
of Kopriv-shtitsa, shall we
sing of the pity in the eyes
of St Trofim on the charred
icons or shall we sing
the unfathomed the fateful
discords of death
in the museum village
of Kopriv-shtitsa?

2

On spring nights
you can hear the
echo of the battle
fought on the bridge
a hundred years ago
in the museum village
of Kopriv-shtitsa.

On spring nights
you can smell the
whispering fear of
the informer and on
spring nights you
can hear the faraway
sound of his horse's
hooves as he rides and
rides into the dawn
of his betrayal.

3

And always
when spring shakes out
its apple blossoms
on the museum roofs
of Kopriv-shtitsa
you can see the mother
who waits still and
dumb as stone in the
forests outside the
museum village of
Kopriv-shtitsa.

She sits there
among the daffodils,
a statue in the forest;
locked into her stone
body with her hand under
her chin, she meditates
and waits for her son
to come back from the
battle he fought
on the bridge outside
the museum village
of Kopriv-shtitsa.

4

She waits for her son
who never comes home
from the Turkish prison,
her son sits there
writing his testament
his renunciation and his
farewell with his own
heart's blood.

His heart is
red as a flower
and death flowers
in his heart until
out of his heart's
blood the red flower
bursts into death,
death that blinds and
burns the mother.

She sits still and
dumb as stone in
the forest outside
the museum village
of Kopriv-shtitsa,
she meditates among
the lichens and mosses;
locked into the stone
of her statue she never
stops waiting for her
son to come home.

5

Inside the museum
we file past mouldering
archives, we stare at
long lists of names in
cyrillic alphabet but
the letters are mute
and motionless, they stay
enshrined in their
glass cases.

We scan row after row
of faces in photographs
as if looking for a
brother, an uncle, or
a dead grandfather,
we recognize no one;
there is no face here
that speaks to us—
there is no sign.

There are only the
tombstones out there
in the forest;
rooted in the bodies
of long-dead warriors
they flower silently
and lean into a future
full of questions.

6

Death flowers and
meditates
and the stone woman
in the statue
sits and grieves
for her son and
his ragged armies.

7

Sometimes they step down
from their photographs,
all the ragged young men
from the peaceful villages,
you can hear their ghosts
riding out on the wind,
you can hear their voices
singing into the trees
rising above the darkness.

8

The past is always
singing and crying
in the green light
of the forest outside
the museum village
of Kopriv-shtitsa,
the past is always
singing and murmuring,
the past is reminding
us to never forget
the battle outside
the museum village
of Kopriv-shtitsa.

WAKE-UP SONG

Lay aside your grief,
old child, infant lady,
in the land of unbelief
grief is the kind of fury

That morning will not bury,
and night cannot erase,
for grief is the weaker side
of anger's double face.

So close accounts at last,
the ill that's done is done,
change the worst to best,
for so must every one.

Now lay aside your grief
and wake the sleepy world,
old child, infant lady—
its yawn is purest gold.